A BOOK of MONKEYS
(AND OTHER PRIMATES)

Katie Viggers

Laurence King Publishing

For team Huggers

LAURENCE KING

Contents

Meet the primates 4

Gorillas 6

Chimpanzees and bonobos 8

Orangutans 10

Gibbons 12

Old World monkeys 14

Baboons, drills and mandrills 16

New World monkeys 18

Howler monkeys 20

Tarsiers, lorises and bushbabies 22

Aye-ayes and lemurs 24

Eating 26

Intelligence 28

Social life 30

The future 32

Meet the primates

We share our planet with more than 400 different species of primate. They range in size from the smallest monkey, the pygmy marmoset, to the largest ape, the gorilla.

Did you know that humans are primates too? In which case, let's meet some of the family!

Us primates don't all live in the same place, we just got together to help make this book.

Gorilla

Orangutan

Chimpanzee

Lemur

Loris

Tarsier

Gibbon

Mandrill

Baboon

Howler monkey

Gorillas

The tropical forests of Africa are home to the gorilla, one of the great apes, and the biggest and strongest of all primates.

Gorillas are very sociable animals and live in family groups with one dominant male and several females.

Scientists think that the male gorilla beats his chest as a warning to rival male gorillas.

MOUNTAIN GORILLA
Gorilla beringei
Mountain gorillas have lots of thick fur. This keeps them warm in their mountain habitat, where temperatures often drop below freezing.

CROSS RIVER GORILLA
Gorilla gorilla diehli
The cross river gorilla lives in the lowland forests of Cameroon and Nigeria and is the rarest ape. It is believed that there are only a few hundred left in the wild today.

Yes, of course this is my natural hair colour!

SILVERBACK
From the age of 12, male gorillas are known as 'silverbacks' because they develop a silver coating of hair over their back and hips. There is normally only one dominant silverback in a family group.

Chimpanzees and bonobos

Chimpanzees and bonobos are our closest living relatives!

These great apes can be found in central and western Africa. Until around 100 years ago, scientists thought these apes were the same species as they look so similar to each other.

CHIMPANZEE
Pan troglodytes
The forests and grasslands of central and western Africa are home to around 300,000 chimpanzees. They live in sociable communities led by a dominant male.

BONOBO
Pan paniscus
Bonobos can only be found in one area in the Democratic Republic of the Congo. They are quite chilled out compared to their lively chimpanzee cousins, and females are usually the ones in charge. It is believed that here are fewer than 20,000 bonobos left in the wild today.

Chimpanzees are broader and more muscular than bonobos, with larger heads and less fur on their faces. Bonobos are smaller and thinner, with darker faces and more fur.

Sticks are good for getting at insects, but a drill would be even better!

Chimpanzees are one of the few species of animal known to use tools. They use sticks to dig out insects and stones to smash open nuts.

Orangutans

In the Malay language, orangutan means 'person of the forest'.

Orangutans are another of the great apes, and they are found on the islands of Sumatra and Borneo in Indonesia.

SUMATRAN ORANGUTAN

Pongo abelii

There are around 13,500 Sumatran orangutans in the wild. Although some do live in small social groups, the males typically live alone and the females live with their offspring.

BORNEAN ORANGUTAN

Pongo pygmaeus

Bornean orangutans are more likely than their Sumatran cousins to spend some time on the ground. There are also many more of them – between 45,000 and 60,000 in the wild.

A third species was recently discovered in Sumatra, called the Tapanuli. It is extremely rare.

It's amazing what you can see from up here. Cooo-eeee!

Orangutans prefer to spend most of their time in the trees, where they feed, sleep, play and just hang around.

FLANGES

As the male orangutans get older, their cheek pads swell and grow. These are called flanges. The bigger the flanges the more attractive they are to females and scarier to other adult males.

Gibbons

Gibbons are known as lesser apes because they're much smaller than their relatives, the great apes.

There are about 20 different species of gibbon in the world, and they all live in the rainforests of Southeast Asia. Most species of gibbon mate for life and live in small family groups.

Gibbons are the fastest of the apes when travelling through treetops. They swing 10 to 15 m between trees at speeds of up to 55 kmph.

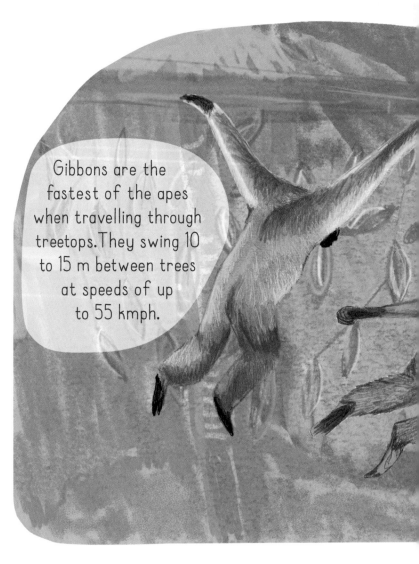

LAR GIBBON
Hylobates lar
The lar, or white-handed gibbon is one of the smallest gibbons. It has soft, thick fur, which varies in colour. All lar gibbons have white hands and feet.

SIAMANG GIBBON
Symphalangus syndactylus
The largest of the gibbons, this stocky ape has shaggy, black fur and a bare throat pouch that inflates when it is calling.

PILIATED GIBBONS
Hylobates pileatus
These gibbons mate for life and form strong bonds with their partners and children.

Aim high! I'm going for gold in the primate Olympics!

A gibbon has hooked hands that are perfect for grabbing on to branches and long arms suited for swinging swiftly through the trees.

Gibbons can walk on two legs for short distances. They hold their arms up in the air to balance themselves.

Old World monkeys

Old World monkeys are found mostly in Africa and Asia. Most have tails, but they don't grip, so Old World monkeys can't use them for swinging between trees.

DE BRAZZA'S MONKEY
Cercopithecus neglectus

De Brazza's monkeys live in the swamp forests and wetlands of central Africa. They have distinctive sad-looking faces and are good swimmers!

COLOBUS MONKEY
Colobus guereza

The striking black-and-white colobus monkey lives in central and east Africa. Unlike other monkeys, they don't have thumbs.

GOLDEN LANGUR
Trachypithecus geei

With its spectacular golden fur, this shy creature is one of the most endangered primates. It is found along the border between India and Bhutan.

TALAPOIN MONKEY
Miopithecus talapoin

The African talapoin monkey is the smallest Old World monkey. Females are just 28 cm long.

CRESTED BLACK MACAQUE
Macaca nigra

The crested black macaque is also known as the Celebes crested macaque because it lives on the island of Celebes in Indonesia.

GOLDEN SNUB-NOSED MONKEY
Rhinopithecus roxellana

This monkey lives in the cold, snowy forests of southwestern China. Its unusual pale blue face looks good against its beautiful, thick, golden fur.

RED-SHANKED DOUC
Pygathrix nemaeus

These slender monkeys live in Laos, Cambodia and Vietnam and have the most unusual maroon-coloured legs.

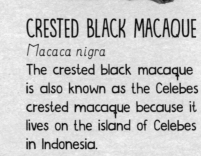

CAT BA LANGUR
Trachypithecus poliocephalus

This golden-headed primate lives on Cát Bà island in Vietnam. There are only around 70 left in the wild.

PROBOSCIS MONKEY
Nasalis larvatus

The proboscis monkey lives in Borneo around wetlands, swamps and mangrove forests. Adult males' noses hang down over their mouths. Scientists aren't sure of the nose's exact function (other than looking funny!), but males can use it to produce loud honking calls, perhaps to attract female mates or to scare rivals away.

JAPANESE MACAQUE
Macaca fuscata

Japanese macaques spend much of their time in the snowy mountains on three of Japan's main islands. They have a thick coat of fur that keeps them toasty warm, but they also like to warm up and relax in hot springs.

Baboons, drills and mandrills

Baboons, drills and mandrills all belong to the Old World Monkey group and they are the largest of all the monkeys.

They all have similar features, but baboons are a different species from drills and mandrills.

HAMADRYAS BABOON
Papio hamadryas
Hamadryas baboons live in northeast Africa. They have been known to gather in large troops of several hundred. That's a lot of monkeys!

MANDRILL
Mandrillus sphinx
The mandrill is the largest monkey and lives in the rainforests of equatorial Africa. Adult males have distinctive blue and red faces, while the females are smaller and have brown faces.

DRILL
Mandrillus leucophaeus
Despite being one of the world's largest monkeys, drills are very shy creatures. They live in the rainforests of Cameroon, Nigeria and Bioko island, Equatorial Guinea and they are endangered.

TEETH
Baboons have large, sharp canine teeth in their top and bottom jaw. These can grow up to 5 cm long. They use them to help them kill and eat their prey, which includes rodents and young antelopes, and to scare off rival males and defend their territory.

When a female chacma baboon is ready to mate, her bottom swells and turns a much brighter red.

The male hamadryas baboon has a thick cape of silvery hair on its neck and shoulders but a completely bald bright-pink bottom.

Drills and mandrills have vibrantly coloured bottoms, in pretty shades of pink, purple and blue. The colour of the males' rumps gets brighter as they move up the ranks of importance within their group.

Can you paint my face blue like my dad's?

This shade of purple looks good on you!

PAINT

Young mandrills and baboons don't have lovely colourful faces or bottoms. The colours only develop as they mature into adults.

New World monkeys

New World monkeys are found in the tropical regions of South America, Central America and Mexico. Unlike Old World monkeys, most have a long tail that can grasp branches like a hand.

BROWN TITI MONKEY
Plecturocebus brunneus

Titi monkeys live in pairs. The male usually carries the baby for a couple of weeks after it's born and this strengthens their bond.

EMPEROR TAMARIN
Saguinus imperator

The emperor tamarin is known for its exceptional moustache and long red-brown tail. It lives in the Amazonian rainforests of Peru, Colombia, Brazil and Bolivia.

SAKI
Pithecia

Saki monkeys sleep curled up like cats in the branches of trees in their rainforest homes in Central and South America.

GOLDEN LION TAMARIN
Leontopithecus rosalia

The golden lion tamarin lives in forests on the Atlantic coast of Brazil. It has a gold, silky mane just like a male lion. It sleeps in tree hollows and feeds on fruit, nectar, insects, grubs and small invertebrates.

UAKARI MONKEY
Cacajao

The uakari monkey is easy to recognise with its bold red face and thick fur. They are small with short stumpy tails.

PYGMY MARMOSET
Cebuella pygmaea

The pygmy marmoset is tiny - about the size of a mouse. It lives in the treetops in the Amazonian rainforests of Peru, Brazil, Colombia and Ecuador.

SPIDER MONKEY
Ateles

There are seven different species of spider monkey. These extremely acrobatic New World monkeys are named after spiders because of the way in which they hang from branches with their long graceful limbs and their flexible prehensile tail, which works just like another arm.

Incy, wincy spider, climbing up the . . . rainforest tree!

CAPUCHIN MONKEY
Cebus

The capuchin monkey is one of the most intelligent of the New World monkeys. It's known for being extremely sociable and using tools to forage for food. It is found in the tropical forests of Central and South America.

WOOLLY MONKEY
Lagothrix

This monkey is one of the largest by weight of the New World monkeys. It has very long arms, legs and a prehensile tail, which allows it to jump and glide easily through the trees of its South American rainforest home. They are not made of wool!

I do hope I can get this scarf finished in time for Lilly's birthday.

SQUIRREL MONKEY
Saimiri

Squirrel monkeys don't really look like squirrels, but they move in a similar way. Their tail is for balance only, they can't wrap it around trees like other New World monkeys can.

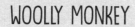

Howler monkeys

Howler monkeys are one of the largest – and the loudest – New World monkeys.

There are around 14 species of howler monkey, ranging in colour from black or brown to beige or red. They live mostly in the tropical forests of Central and South America.

BLACK HOWLER MONKEY

Alouatta caraya

These large primates have grasping five-toed feet and a prehensile (able to hold on to things) tail, which helps them move around the trees.

Howler monkeys know how to get themselves heard – they make a deep barking sound. Their call is so loud it can be heard up to 5 km away!

Did you know that black howler monkeys are born with beige fur? As males grow, their fur turns black, but the females stay beige. They are one of the few primates where males and females have different coloured fur.

JUST CHILLING

Howler monkeys have to eat a lot to feed their large bodies. To conserve their energy, they spend a lot of time just chilling in the trees.

Tarsiers, lorises and bushbabies

These tiny nocturnal primates have huge eyes to help them see at night.

Tarsiers, lorises and bushbabies live in different parts of the world, but they have many behavioural and physical similarities.

TARSIER
Tarsiidae

Tarsiers live in the tropical forests of Southeast Asia. They have excellent hearing, which helps them to locate their prey in the dark.

LORIS
Lorisidae

There are 11 known species of slow loris and slender loris in the forests of Southeast Asia. They often hang by their feet to free their hands for foraging.

BUSHBABY
Galagidae

Bushbabies live in parts of Africa. They have special skin on their paws that acts like suckers to give them a stronger grip.

The Javan slow loris has a very strong back, which is handy as it often hangs upside down by its feet.

POTTO
Lorisidae

Pottos belongs to the same family as the loris but live in Africa. With their woolly fur and small stubby ears, this primate is also sometimes called a 'tree bear'.

Bushbabies smear wee on their hands and feet so they can retrace their steps using the scent left on the branches.

Slender lorises almost never come down to the ground. They prefer to stay high up in the safety of the trees.

Bushbabies and tarsiers are very good at leaping. They can jump around 5 m from one tree to another!

DJ Tarsier in the forest!

I am pretty sure I can see the Monkey Head Nebula up there . . .

Night-time is when all these tiny primates come alive. It's the best time for them to forage for food and to socialise – and maybe even do a spot of stargazing or dancing.

Aye-ayes and lemurs

Over 100 species of aye-aye and lemur live on the island of Madagascar. Lemurs cannot be found anywhere else in the world!

Unlike most primates, female lemurs are the ones in charge. They generally get to eat first and choose their mates. Females sit high in the trees to get the best food, while males sit lower down and wait their turn to eat.

The indri is one of the largest lemurs. It has big hands and feet, and with its strong, long hind legs, it can jump up to 10 m between branches.

RING-TAILED LEMUR
Lemur catta
The ring-tailed lemur is instantly recognised by its stripy tail. They enjoy walking around on the floor as much as hanging out in trees.

MOUSE LEMUR
Microcebus murinus
This is one of the smallest primates in the world. They spend their days sleeping but are very active at night, running and jumping through the trees.

AYE-AYE
Daubentonia madagascariensis
The aye-aye is the largest of the nocturnal primates – and one of the most spooky looking! Its teeth are very powerful, and its big bushy tail helps it to balance whilst walking in the trees.

Eating

Most primates eat mainly fruit, vegetables, shoots, nuts and sometimes meat. This makes them omnivorous – which means they eat both meat and plant-based food. Primates have to eat whatever fruits and vegetables are in season where they live.

Spider monkeys mostly eat fruits and seeds, but they will occasionally snack on leaves, flowers and insects, too.

Mandrills are omnivores and will eat a wide variety of fruit, vegetables, insects, small lizards and frogs.

Tarsiers are the only primate that doesn't eat any plant matter at all. They feast on insects, frogs, mice and grubs. Yum!

Chimpanzees eat fruit, plants, eggs and will also sometimes eat meat. But their favourite food is figs. They eat a LOT of figs!

Slow lorises love a bit of tree sap but are also partial to an insect or two.

Capuchins will fish for clams and frogs, but they also eat insects and a variety of nuts and fruits. They have terrible table manners.

Gibbons love berries.
They will also eat leaves
if the fruit is scarce.
They are not fussy.

Orangutans enjoy
eating the smelly durian
fruit that grows in Indonesia.
Babies drink their mother's
milk for up to eight years.
(It takes them that long to
have the courage to even try
the stinky durian.)

Gorillas like to eat – a lot!
An adult gorilla can eat
up to 30 kg of food each
day! Mountain gorillas can
spend up to six hours
a day eating.

Lemurs love the leaves
and fruits of the tamarind
tree that grows in Madagascar.

Intelligence

Primates don't always get their meals served to them at a table. They have to use their skills and brain power to find food and survive life in the wild.

The clever long-tailed macaque lives in Southeast Asia. Those that live by the sea have learned how to use stones to open clam, oyster and crab shells, earning them the name 'crab-eating macaques'.

SMASHING CLASS

1. Find a big rock
2. Lift above your head
3. Hit shell with rock
4. Eat

Who needs a stick when you can use a power tool?!

It was once believed that only humans made and used tools, but the highly intelligent chimpanzee has been spotted stripping leaves off branches and using the sticks as tools.

Chimpanzees use sticks to get honey or insects out of hollows in trees.

Capuchins are extremely intelligent monkeys, who learn by watching their elders. This is how they learn to smash open tasty palm nuts with rocks!

It's a skill that requires strength...

precision and patience...

...but is worth it!

Orangutans have been known to recognise their own reflection in water.

Chimpanzees in Guinea, Africa, have been spotted using sticks to scoop up algae to eat.

This clever orangutan is using the stick to test the depth of the water. Maybe she could go for a dip if it's not too deep?

Social life

Primates are chatty creatures, and have a range of ways to communicate with each other – pretty much like us humans! Communication helps them to form strong bonds within their social groups.

Apes can communicate using hand gestures. (They don't actually wave like this gorilla though!) The gestures include things such as a tap on the shoulder for attention or an outstretched hand to ask for food.

The little vervet monkey is a great communicator and has a range of squeals to alert its friends to different types of danger. They have a call that warns the group to look up for eagles and one that tells them to look down for snakes!

GROOMING

Grooming is hugely important to most primates, and it plays a big part in their group interactions. They groom to show love, trust and appreciation, as well as finding tasty little lice to eat!

Infants will groom their elders.

Females will groom males.

Females will groom their infants.

The black crested macaque is one of the most affectionate monkeys. They will cuddle to simply make friends. Macaques show their lips to let other macaques know that they would like a cuddle.

The titi monkey cuddles using its tail. To feel close to one another, the monkeys twist their tails together. This strenghtens their bond and also helps them balance whilst sleeping on a branch.

Japanese macaques live in very cold conditions. To keep warm, they work together and form a huddle. This way, they get to share their body heat and stay toasty.

Friends will groom friends.

Lemurs like to groom each other but use their tongues to groom, a bit like cats.

The future

The threat to any endangered primate is mainly due to the loss of their habitats, but that is not the only problem that they face.

Some primates, such as the Cat Ba langur, have come close to extinction due to hunting. Efforts are now being made to protect both them and their habitats.

I am not a pet; I am WILD!

The slow loris is often taken from the wild to be sold as a pet, when they should be roaming free in the forests.

The removal of the tropical forests in favour of palm oil plantations has been devastating for the Sumatran orangutan.

By protecting the places where orangutans, gorillas and other primates live, we can make sure they all have a safe future.